Anthems and Choral Songs

for upper-voice choirs

(sopranos and altos, and/or boys' unchanged voices)

MUSIC DEPARTMENT

OXFORD

UNIVERSITY PRESS

OXFORD
UNIVERSITY PRESS

Great Clarendon Street, Oxford OX2 6DP,
United Kingdom

Oxford University Press is a department of the University of Oxford.
It furthers the University's objective of excellence in research, scholarship,
and education by publishing worldwide. Oxford is a registered trade mark of
Oxford University Press in the UK and in certain other countries

First published 2019

Impression: 1

ISBN 978-0-19-353023-2

Music originated on Sibelius
Printed in Great Britain on acid-free paper by
Halstan & Co. Ltd, Amersham, Bucks.

Contents

for Clare College, Cambridge

A Clare Benediction

Words and music by
JOHN RUTTER

you; may his spi - rit be ev-er by your side._____ When you

sleep, may his an - gels watch o - ver you;_____ when you

wake, may he fill you with his grace:_____ May you

love him and serve him all your_ days, Then in

love him and serve_____ him all your days,_____

in memory of the victims of the Tohoku area earthquake and tsunami, March 2011

A flower remembered

Words and music by
JOHN RUTTER

Also published in its original version for mixed voices (978-0-19-340482-3)

*or other vocalized sound, like 'Ah' or 'Oo'

A Gaelic Blessing

Words by William Sharp (1855–1905)
adapted by JR

JOHN RUTTER

*If preferred, these four bars may be sung an octave higher.

light_____ on you,   Deep   peace_____ of

light_____ on you,   Deep   peace_____ of

Deep   peace_____ of_____

Christ,_____   of_____ Christ_____ the_____

Christ,_____   of_____ Christ_____ the

Christ,_____   of_____ Christ_____ the_____

light_____ of the world to you,_____

light_____ of the world to you,_____

light_____ of the world to you,

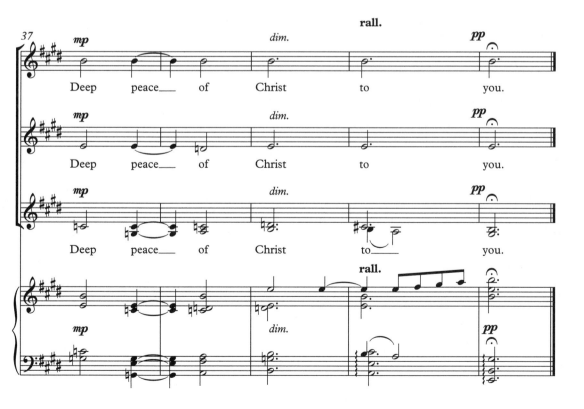

Deep peace___ of Christ to you.

Deep peace___ of Christ to you.

Deep peace___ of Christ to___ you.

Commissioned by Westminster Choir College for Helen Kemp

All things bright and beautiful

Words by Mrs C. F. Alexander (1823–95)

JOHN RUTTER

purple-head-ed moun-tain, The riv-er run-ning by, The

sun-set, and the morn-ing___ That bright-ens up___ the___ sky;___

ALTOS
___ The cold wind___ in the win-ter,___ The plea-sant sum-mer sun,___

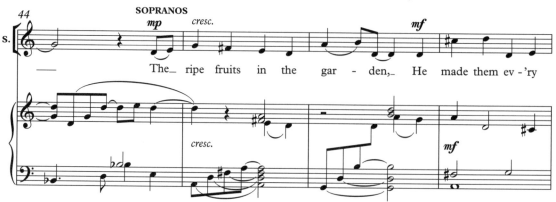

SOPRANOS
S. ___ The___ ripe fruits in the gar-den,___ He made them ev-'ry

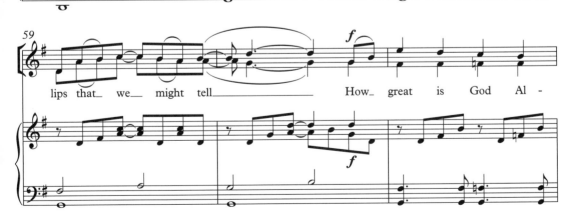

Commissioned by the Texas Choral Directors' Association

For the beauty of the earth

Words by F. S. Pierpoint (1835–1917)

JOHN RUTTER

love_____ which from our birth_____ O-ver and a-

-round us lies,_____ o-ver and a-round us lies:_____ Lord of

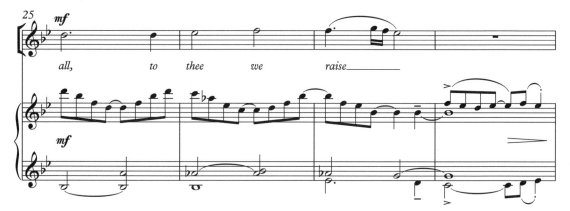

all,   to   thee   we   raise_____

*This our joy - ful hymn__   of   praise.*_____

Lord of all,   to thee   we

stars   of light:_____   Lord of   all,   to   thee   we_____

cresc.

raise_____   This   our joy - ful hymn____   of

raise_____   This_____   our hymn of

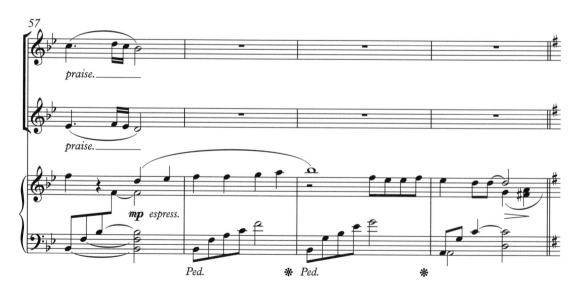

praise._____

praise._____

Ped.   ✻ Ped.   ✻

4. For each per - fect gift of thine_____

To our race so free - ly giv - en,_____ Gra - ces

Gra - ces_____ hu-man and di - vine,_____

hu - - man and di - vine,_____ Flow'rs of earth and

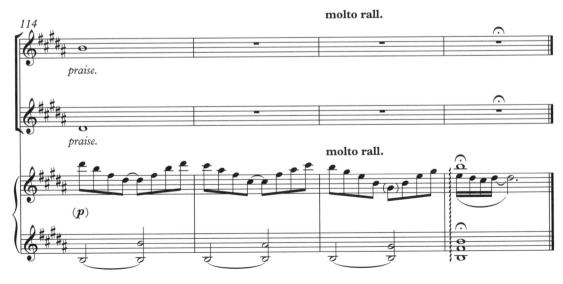

God be in my head

Words from the Sarum Primer (1514)

JOHN RUTTER

in celebration of the 70th anniversary of the Council for the Protection of Rural England

Look at the world

Words and music by
JOHN RUTTER

SOPRANOS 1 and 2

1. Look at the world, ev - 'ry-thing all a - round us:
2. Look at the earth bring-ing forth fruit and flow - er;

Look at the world,___ and mar - vel ev - 'ry day.
Look at the sky,___ the sun - shine and the rain;

Look at the world: so ma-ny joys and won-ders,
Look at the hills, look at the trees and moun-tains,

So ma-ny mi - ra - cles a - long our way.
Val-ley and flow - ing ri - ver, field and plain:

A

SOPRANO 1
mf
S.1
Praise to thee, O Lord, for all cre - a - tion,

SOPRANO 2
mf
S.2
Praise to thee, O Lord, for all cre - a - tion,

ALTO
mf
A.
Praise to thee, O Lord, for all___ cre - a - tion,

A

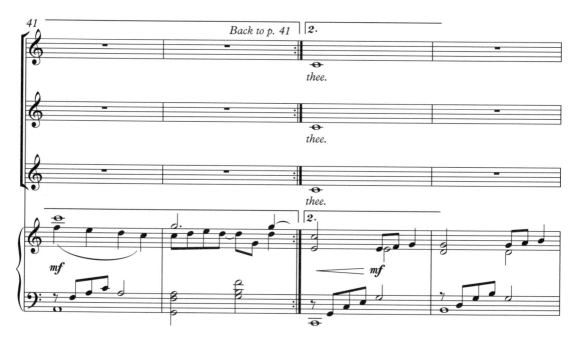

*Small notes are for rehearsal only.

ev - 'ry   bless - ing,   All   things_____   come   of   thee.

ev - 'ry   bless - ing,   All   things_____   come   of   thee.

ev - 'ry   bless - ing,   All   things_____   come   of   thee.

D   **SOPRANOS and ALTOS**

4. Ev-'ry good

gift,   all that we   need   and   che - rish

Comes from the Lord____ in to - ken of his

love; We are his hands,

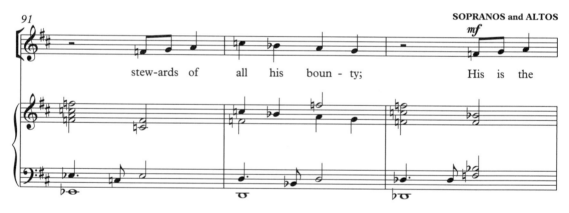

stew-ards of all his boun - ty; His is the

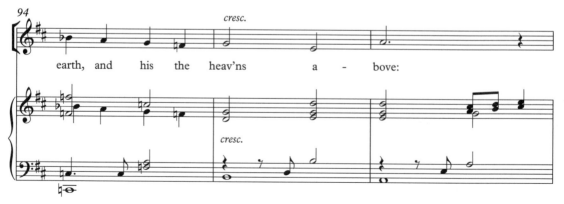

earth, and his the heav'ns a - bove:

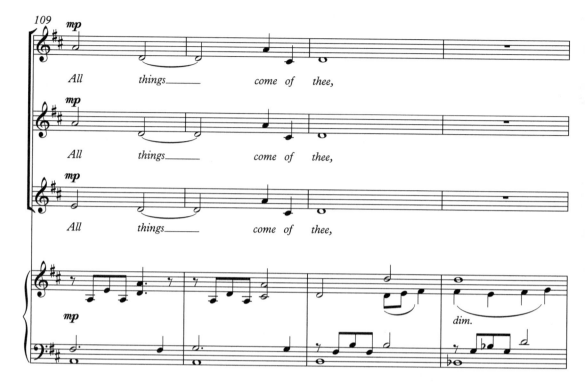

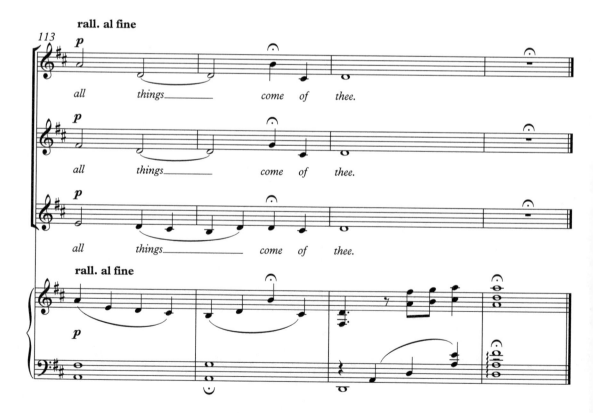

The Lord bless you and keep you

Numbers 6: 24

JOHN RUTTER

for Per-Anders Sjöberg and friends

The Music's Always There With You

Words and music by
JOHN RUTTER

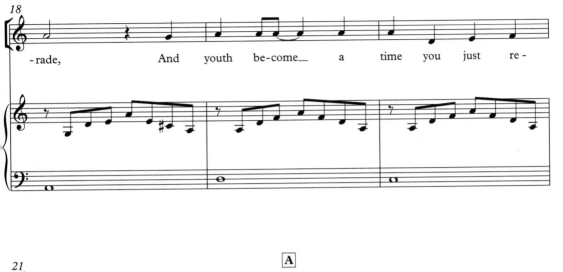

-rade,   And   youth be-come___   a   time   you   just   re-

-call;_____   But the good times   to - geth - er   seem so

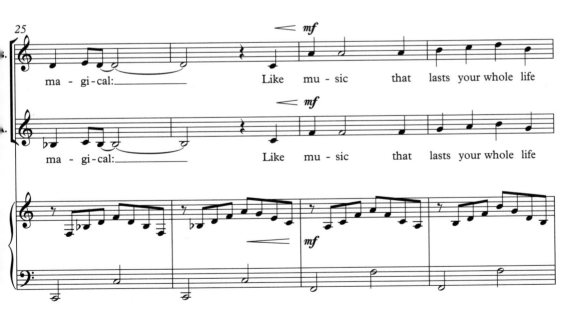

ma - gi - cal:_____   Like   mu - sic   that   lasts your whole life

ma - gi - cal:_____   Like   mu - sic   that   lasts your whole life

'Cos the music's always there in your heart. But the magic you share when you make music. Won't

77

leave you   when the time has come to   part:_____   And it

mp

leave you   when the time has come to   part:_____   And it

mp

leave you   when the time has come to   part:_____

leave you   when the time has come to   part:_____

⌐ 3 ⌐

dim.

81   **Freely**   **rall.**

feels like   you   nev - er have to   say   good - bye,

feels like   you   nev - er have to   say   good - bye,

mp

Oo_____   'Cos the

mp

Oo_____   'Cos the

Freely   **rall.**

mp